# recipe for a
# happy life

# recipe for a
# happy life

## Cheryl Saban Ph.D

RYLAND
PETERS
& SMALL
LONDON NEW YORK

DESIGNER Iona Hoyle
COMMISSIONING EDITOR
Annabel Morgan
PICTURE RESEARCH Emily Westlake
PRODUCTION Maria Petalidou
ART DIRECTOR Leslie Harrington
PUBLISHING DIRECTOR Alison Starling

First published in 2010 by
Ryland Peters & Small
20–21 Jockey's Fields
London WC1R 4BW
and
519 Broadway, Fifth Floor
New York, NY 10012
www.rylandpeters.com

Text copyright © Cheryl Saban 2010
Design and illustrations copyright
© Ryland Peters & Small 2010

10 9 8 7 6 5 4

ISBN 978-1-84597-945-4
Printed and bound in China.

RPS
CICO
BOOKS

For digital editions visit
www.rylandpeters.com/apps.php

# contents

*Man is fond of counting his troubles, but he does not count his joys.*
*If he counted them up as he ought to, he would see that every lot*
*has enough happiness provided for it.*

FYODOR DOSTOEVSKY

# introduction

In this day and age, it's easy to understand why people get sad or feel overwhelmed. How does one cope with financial woes, marital strife, and health problems? Where does hope come from, after all? Can we be happy despite the difficult life-cards we've been dealt?

The answer—though difficult to fathom—is yes. Some studies suggest that our ability to be happy is partly genetic, partly environmental, and partly due to personal intention. In other words, a major proportion of your ability to be happy is entirely up to you, so make it your intention to be happy!

Ultimately, all of us yearn for happiness. Though we struggle with difficult challenges, we have it within us to make the best of our lives. Believe that you can. Hope is a mighty motivator and, as they say, hope floats. I invite you to float your own boat, see your cup as half-full, and view your struggles as opportunities to learn, change and grow. Attract positive experiences into your life by choosing to be happy, despite life's troubles.

Happiness is contagious. Spread it around generously to your mate, your family members, and your friends. Create your own recipe for a happy life. Season it with love, compassion, and positive intentions, and you can enjoy a lifetime of contentment and fulfilment—starting right now!

recipe for a
*happy life*

*be optimistic* ✸ NOURISH CLOSE RELATIONSHIPS

*be content with who you are*

HAVE GOALS AND AMBITIONS ✸ *be grateful*

*give to others* ✸ DISCOVER YOUR PASSIONS

*practice random acts of kindness*

IMPROVE YOUR TALENTS ✸ *be kind and encouraging*

*forgive others and yourself* ✸ TAKE REGULAR EXERCISE

*mind your health and take care of yourself*

✸ NURTURE YOUR SPIRITUAL BELIEFS ✸

*attract positive experiences* ✸ *know your self-worth*

✸ EAT REASONABLY AND SLEEP DEEPLY ✸

*pray* ✸ WRITE YOUR STORY ✸ *commune with nature*

✸ LEARN POSITIVE COPING SKILLS ✸

*write in a journal* ✸ EXPRESS GOOD INTENTIONS

*meditate* ✸ *laugh more* ✸ LOVE ✸ *choose happiness*

*Happiness is when what you think, what you say,*
*and what you do are in harmony.*

**MOHANDAS K. GANDHI**

# *connections*

COMMUNICATE ❊ UNITY ❊ COMMUNITY

Connections are important in every aspect of life. Connect to yourself, to nature, to God, and to others. Strive to form close, strong relationships with family members, friends, and colleagues. Fuel your passions, and find your soul mate.

Give love, create love, and receive love. Embrace commitment—feelings of permanence, longevity, and stability are important ingredients in a successful relationship. And remember that healthy, close, and supportive relationships will only serve to enrich your life, bring you joy, and make you feel happy!

An honest assessment of your innermost feelings and beliefs will help you live an authentic life. When you know yourself, you're more able to connect with others. Engage in physical activities, look after your health, and nurture your friendships. Discover your passions and hidden talents and share them with others. Count your blessings and develop an appreciation of the special beauty that is present in even the most mundane and everyday things.

Turn wishful thinking into positive action.
Those who take a proactive stance in their lives
tend to have an ample supply of joy and pleasure.

*Twenty years from now you will be more disappointed by the things that you didn't do than by the ones you did do. So throw off the bowlines. Sail away from the safe harbor. Catch the trade winds in your sails. Explore. Dream. Discover.*

MARK TWAIN

Choose your friends wisely, and then enjoy them for who they are. Anxiety about your social status can affect your happiness quotient—and what's the point of that?

*Let us be grateful to people who make us happy;*
*they are the charming gardeners*
*who make our souls blossom.*

MARCEL PROUST

*There is only one happiness in life,*
*to love and be loved.*

GEORGE SAND

Try to make at least three people
smile each day—beginning with yourself!

Seek positive role models and learn
life-enhancing, esteem-building
behaviors from them.

*A friend is a gift
you give yourself.*

ROBERT LOUIS STEVENSON

Remember the Law of Attraction, and make an effort to attract positive, happy experiences into your life

*The happiness of your life depends
on the quality of your thoughts.*

MARCUS AURELIUS ANTONINUS

*It is neither wealth nor splendor; but tranquility*
*and occupation which give you happiness.*

THOMAS JEFFERSON

Be true to yourself—be authentic.
Live your life according to your
deeply held values.
It will make you feel better.

Engage in a positive internal conversation.
Write in a journal, and tell yourself encouraging
and supportive stories about being you.

*Independence is happiness.*

SUSAN B. ANTHONY

*The richness I achieve comes from Nature,*
*the source of my inspiration.*

CLAUDE MONET

# *wellbeing*

MEDITATE ✤ DE-STRESS ✤ REJUVENATE

Take good care of yourself, mind and body. Take exercise—just thirty minutes a day will sharpen your problem-solving skills, and help to keep your body functioning to the best of its ability.

You can exercise your mind, too, by continuing to learn. Have faith in your ability to develop new skills, and learn from every experience, especially the challenging ones. Resist helplessness or blind acceptance of unpleasant circumstances. Although you can't change the facts of your life, you can change your perspective on those facts! A relaxed mental state will allow you to have an awareness of the present moment. And that, after all, is all we have.

Take responsibility for the quality of your life, and find a reason to enjoy every day. Be creative, and look for ways to be inspired.

Master a new skill.
When you take the time to engage in activities that
absorb your full attention, you'll experience a sense of
well-being and contentment.

*Live as if you were to die tomorrow.*
*Learn as if you were to live forever.*

MOHANDAS K. GANDHI

Live your life fully now.
This is not a dress rehearsal.
Use it before you lose it!

*The foolish man seeks happiness in the distance,*
*the wise grows it under his feet.*

JAMES OPPENHEIM

*The greatest part of our happiness depends on
our dispositions, not our circumstances.*

MARTHA WASHINGTON

Use your natural gifts and talents.
Find ways to enhance your quality
of life with them.

Find your center—
a calm and content place deep
inside yourself—and spend
some time there each day.

*Hope is the thing with feathers—*
*that perches in the soul—*
*and sings the tune—without the words—*
*and never stops at all.*

**EMILY DICKINSON**

Avoid false fixes.
Over-indulging in shopping, food, alcohol, or drugs
won't bring you happiness. Ask for help—
and seek positive coping skills instead.

*Wisdom is the supreme part of happiness.*

SOPHOCLES

*Happiness comes when your work and words
are of benefit to yourself and others.*

**BUDDHA**

Take pleasure in the positive, and find
constructive ways to mitigate the negative.

Laugh out loud, robustly and often.
No one is in charge of your happiness but you!

*If only we'd stop trying to be happy*
*we'd have a pretty good time.*

EDITH WHARTON

Be willing to live life to your fullest potential, and believe in the fact that you have plenty of it.

*Our greatest happiness does not depend on the condition of life in which chance has placed us, but is always the result of a good conscience, good health, occupation, and freedom in all just pursuits.*

THOMAS JEFFERSON

*Fill the cup of happiness for others, and there will be enough overflowing to fill yours to the brim.*

ROSE PASTOR STOKES

# gratitude

GIVE THANKS ❧ ACKNOWLEDGE BLESSINGS ❧ HELP OTHERS

Be grateful for the blessings you have, and at the same time be happy for others. This is not a competition—there is plenty of happiness to go around, once you know where to look. And besides, happiness is contagious, so make an effort to infect everyone around you.

Focus on the quality of your life, rather than the quantity—there are no guarantees. Look around you. Enjoy the simple yet miraculous things life has to offer. Find pleasure in the sunrise, and amazement in the moonlight. Be thrilled by the miracle of birth, and respectful of the power of nature. Be cognizant of the flora and fauna that exists on this earth, and appreciate the very air you breathe. Inhale the fragrance of flowers, and delight in the shade thrown by a tree. Perform random acts of kindness. You'll discover that gratitude and forgiveness are essential ingredients of a happy and fulfilled life.

Be grateful. A sense of gratitude for life and the blessings you've been given can help you keep things in perspective when you hit a bump in the road.

*We don't receive wisdom; we must discover it for ourselves after a journey that no one can take for us or spare us.*

MARCEL PROUST

Give of your time, talent, and treasure to others in need,
and practice random acts of kindness. These rewarding
activities will make you feel really good!

*The happiest people I know have been those who gave themselves*
*no concern about their own souls, but did their uttermost*
*to mitigate the miseries of others.*

ELIZABETH CADY STANTON

Forgive. No matter how good or bad a situation is, it will change. Be willing to adapt.

*Forget the past and live the present hour.*

SARAH KNOWLES BOLTON

Sing and hum. Read stories about triumph over catastrophe, of growth, progress, and change for the better.

*Always be a little kinder than necessary.*

JAMES M. BARRIE

Eat reasonably, get enough sleep, and walk!
These are simple instructions, but amazingly effective.

*To be what we are, and to become what we are capable of becoming, is the only end of life.*

ROBERT LOUIS STEVENSON

Live your life with thoughtfulness and purpose.
It's up to you, after all.

*The only truly happy man is always a fighting optimist.*
*Optimism includes not only altruism but also social responsibility,*
*social courage, and objectivity.*

W. BERAN WOLFE

Thank God, tell the truth, and be proactive.

*Happiness belongs to the self-sufficient.*

ARISTOTLE

Do the tough stuff. Living an authentic life requires you to make hard choices. Find the courage to be the best you can be.

*Whatever is—is best.*

ELLA WHEELER WILCOX

# photography credits

**MARTIN BRIGDALE**
Page 53.

**PETER CASSIDY**
Pages 39, 43.

**LISA COHEN**
Page 48, 49.

**CHRIS EVERARD**
Page 42.

**JONATHAN GREGSON**
Page 37.

**TOM LEIGHTON**
Page 20.

**WILLIAM LINGWOOD**
Page 18.

**PAUL MASSEY**
Pages 1 (www.jane-packer.co.uk), 6, 12, 29, 32, 33 (www.tresanton.com), 52 (www.olelynggaard.dk), 55, 59, 61.

**JAMES MERRELL**
Pages 50, 60.

**CLAIRE RICHARDSON**
Pages 3, 9, 14, 17, 19, 21 (www.chambres-provence.com), 25, 26, 31, 36, 40, 44, 57 below, 63-64.

**PAUL RYAN**
Page 13.

**DEBI TRELOAR**
Pages 2, 15, 16, 22, 35, 41, 54, 56, 57 above, 58.

**CHRIS TUBBS**
Page 34.

**POLLY WREFORD**
Pages 4-5, 8, 10, 23, 24, 28, 30, 38, 46, 47, 51, 62.

# acknowledgments

I feel incredibly blessed by the circle of family and friends that surround me.
Though my experience of happiness is in great part up to me, I am honored
to acknowledge and thank the following individuals for adding love,
joy, giggles, support, compassion, and adventure to my life.
I dedicate this book happily, with love, to you.

Haim: my husband, my love, my life-partner.

My children: Tifanie and Chris, and their children, Marley and Griffin;
Heidi and Christopher, and their children, Jaccoa and Sarenne; Ness; Tanya.

My parents: Betty and Ken Flor; my mother-in-law, Virginie Saban.

My brother Ken; my sister Debbie and her husband Doug, and their children,
Ashley and Kelsey; my brother and sister-in-law Arieh and Varda, and their
children, Sigal, Yoni, and Gil.

My girlfriends.